Plagiarism, Plagiarism, Plagiarism

Tom Hodges

Order this book online at www.trafford.com
or email orders@trafford.com

Most Trafford titles are also available at major online book retailers.

Print information available on the last page.

ISBN: 978-1-4907-9914-8 (sc)
ISBN: 978-1-4907-9912-4 (e)

Library of Congress Control Number: 2020900335

Trafford rev. 01/16/2020

www.trafford.com
North America & international
toll-free: 1 888 232 4444 (USA & Canada)
fax: 812 355 4082

Contents

Dedication vii
Thanks... ix

About the Author 1
The Artist 2
Absolute 3
Anti-Ojos 4
Blossom... 5
Conquest.. 6
Dying Cadence 7
Final... 8
Flowers for the Living.. 9
How Far Did the Apple Fall? 10
Imagine... 11
In His Own Heaven... 12
In the Shadow 13
No Benefits 14
An Ode to Living 15
Of Love and Passion.. 16
A Poem about Poetry... 17
Queen 18
Sentiment Is Emotional 19
Sunbeams.. 20
Tender 21
Think... 22
What Do You See? 23
Who Are We?... 24
Silence of the Night... 25

Dedication

To my son, Marc. He introduced me to classical literature.

Thanks

A grateful thanks to two very special people who edited
most of the selection: Mary Hitch and Mary Powell.

Special kudos to my wife, Frances, who is
the "wind beneath my wings."

About the Author

Poet TOM HODGES grew up in Coppell, Texas. Much of his writing sprung from his Texas roots, onward to the American South, and into the rugged mountains of Colorado. Nature left a huge impression on his imagination, which led him to be observant and visionary.

The Artist

Focus on darkness,
   touching night;
bright tunnels seeing
   beyond walls.

Art must be spontaneous
   and imperfect.
Folk songs are born
   from impulse.

Too much knowledge
   diminishes
men's sense
   of wonder.

A delicacy, a beauty
   in all forms—
Like a narcotic
   to all senses.

Morning is full
   of new creations;
Dewdrops falling
   from the sky.

Absolute

Come away—
    the night is young
to touch a flame
    of desire.

A world
    that might be,
not the one
    that is.

Lovely moments
    embrace happiness;
making love
    in the dark.

A flower blossomed
    into bloom,
reflecting shadows
    on the wall.

Anti-Ojos

Look for beauty
    existing all around;
choose extraordinary
    moments.

No past or future—
    destiny is today.
Live the life
    of now.

Blossom

The beauty
   of a woman
excites
   the senses.

A flower
   comes forth
with love's
   innocence.

You have youth
   and a dream
crushed between
   past and future.

Creation's
   silent passion
burns with
   desire.

Touch me, touch me.

Conquest

During the quiet of early morn,
    Where one can think and write,
A silence has been broken
    With echoes of memory.

Adventure drives men.
    The invisible line was crossed
Awash in nostalgia
    With an ocean of images.

Like a maze of certainty,
    Destiny is keeping its appointment.
And like a god,
    He can create life.

Dying Cadence

It was a black night hung
    from a single star.
Darkness awakened the aches
    of yesterday.
Let us not confuse failure
    with defeat.
He drifted through an alcoholic fog,
    vanishing
Back into the womb
    of creation.

She represented the evolution
    of class.
Her body blossomed
    like a flower.
Their presence excited the senses
    and lit a lovely flame.
Beauty and love pass, but light
    Filters through the rain,
Giving way to the luxury
    of tears.

Final

As we walk
    on the world stage,
what can one say
    that has not been said?
You get one chance
    at life;
take it and pass it on.

Here we are with crow's-feet
    and great big ears.
Bags are under our eyes
    as so many of us shuffle
along, depending upon Depends,
    afraid of a fall—afraid of a fall
that's coming.

Yes, the end of that play
    is upon us.
My old friends are leaving
    each passing day
right here—right here in river city.
    How will they be remembered?

Soon, memories will be
    the only thing left.
Did we give our greatest
    performance?
What will be our legacy
    before that black angel
comes around?

Flowers for the Living

By drinking, he numbed
   the edge of perception,
failing to kill
   his loneliness.

Nothing could hurt him,
   for he cared not.
Flowers seemed to doze
   on their stalks.

Separate oneself from judgment
   and criticism.
Be intoxicated
   by the romance of living.

Walk with those
   who need a light,
in search of your place
   under the sun.

How Far Did the Apple Fall?

We take ourselves
    with us
no matter where
    we go.
Children are raised
    by parents
who are their
    only models.
Change evolves slowly,
    and siblings
repeat their
    upbringing.

One must be
    very strong
to challenge a bad
    situation.
Love and discipline
    are subjects taught.
They correct
    moral character.
Buckle up those infants
    in the back seat.
They are the seeds
    for the next generation.

Imagine

Imagine
    not knowing
who you are
    or your children's names.

Imagine
    not knowing
how to love
    or to be loved.

Imagine
    forgetting
how to read, write,
    and talk.

Imagine
    a slow death
before you
    can say goodbye.

In His Own Heaven

Before comfort descended upon him,
    feelings were a mixture of critical wit,
realizing that he was enjoying life.
    Being a supreme egotist, he was
full of radiant curiosity in spite
    of a melodramatic past.

Inspirations come from life, not from art.

Imagination and courage were in close
    harmony, finding a perfect rhythm,
and yet luxury of leisure drove him wild.
    He assumed an ungrateful position in
society, with its mental and physical
    inferiors who bred a defiant attitude.

In the Shadow

We live in a fantasy
   of immortality.
Should the void left
   by religion be filled?

Freedom's independence
   and competition
has given
   perpetual growth.

The Western world dreads
   mental deterioration
and the loss of identity
   that it brings.

Old age offers the prize
   of wisdom,
but if you lose memory,
   has reason been lost?

No Benefits

Women try
   To possess.
A lay isn't enough;
   They want your soul.

Through her
   Angry tears—
Never surrender to
   Emotions.

There can be desire
   Without love.
To overcome
   Is to satisfy.

Immortality allows
   Us to meet

Our parents and children
   In heaven.

Up there are angels
   Flying from cloud to cloud.
There is no beer
   Or sex.

You could run into
   Your ex-lovers
Or your ex-wives
   Or husbands.

Look upon life
   As an adventure.
Great things happen
   To those who take risks.

An Ode to Living

The body withers
   with the skin,
an anger melted
   for a moment.
It was impossible
   to think of once being young.

After drawing in a deep
   breath of pleasure,
Grams and I saw faces
   in a dream
with eyes trembling
   in tears.

Struggling against
   aching silence,
we went to the mirror
   and looked at ourselves …
Old age dried up
   springs of memory.

Of Love and Passion

Both were calm
    and numb
with sexual
    desire.

Time touched
    absolute pleasure,
something beyond
    carnal knowledge.

Each seeking
    gratification—
sensuous lust
    for the body.

A bud blossomed
    into extreme fervor;
she opened her flower
    like a flame.

A passion so intense,
    it was
beyond their
    control.

They played
    with fire,
not the terms
    of endearment.

Warm devotion
    felt by lovers—
an unselfish concern
    for each other.

Romantic love
    born with tenderness,
like a plant that thrives
    in sunshine.

A Poem about Poetry

By nature,
 We are subjective;
People are not affected
 By art the same way.
When you receive a book
 Of metrical writing,
It is the artist's desire
 That you find the beauty
Of expression in meaning,
 Sound, and rhythm.

Poetry is an art form
 Felt rather than seen.
We are asked to take a
 Journey and to explore.
Poets are dreamers surrounded
 By metaphors
Living in a world
 Of imagination.
History would be empty without
 Whitman, Sandberg, and Frost.

Queen

Men who express passion
     won't love you;
he is looking
     for a trophy.

She was never allowed
     to be herself;
love begets love,
     inspired by affection—

With feelings
     short-lived,
distinguished
     from reason.

Oh, how she longed
     for a tender kiss,
like an infant crying
     in the night.

Entangled in powerful
     liberations,
he said,
     "You have beautiful legs."

Sentiment Is Emotional

Touching the spirit of emotion
   running through the soul,
they stepped into the sensuous
   with a curious expression.

Throbbing with sincerity,
   he hid passion
in the corner
   of the mind.

She stood still in quietness
   for a moment
as if he deserted her
   with lingering regret.

They had left
   a part of themselves behind
with a quality
   of eternal reassurance.

The rules of affection
   acted as brakes on desire.
It was a scrapbook of their lives,
   a payment for the loss of youth.

Sunbeams

It is all about words,
    a character in a book,
A living beauty, a light
    at dawn shining.

Morning was full
    of new creations;
The scent of sunshine—
    a life.

She was a pleasure
    to the senses.
Her breasts were keen
    with passion.

Those pretty blue eyes
    were filled with spring.
'Tis better to desire
    than to possess.

Tender

Must you be a savage
    without passion
or a real devil?
    Let life exist.

Struggle through
    the maze of darkness
like a flower unfolding—
    so new, so tender.

You can hear her soul
    crying out.
She wants love—
    pure love.

An apple blossom
    drinking perfume,
feeling so alive
    with images.

A golden light
    is brewing in our cloud—
A flower
    so new, so tender.

Think

He cherished
   solitude
and discovered
   living.

The ideas of faith
   evaporated.
Rebirth lies
   within you.

Scientists sought
   reason;
we make salvation
   and fortunes.

Live a full life
   of the mind;
hold on to that
   thought.

What Do You See?

We see the birth of time
    that is to come—
a vision evolving
    to reality.

We see the chance to design
    a new beginning—
a place that will inspire
    learning.

We see a symbol—
    a hive of creativity,
a road map
    into the future.

Who Are We?

Look for the beauty
    that exists all around us;
choose extraordinary moments
    to find happiness.

Everyone is chasing success
    rather than greatness.
We choose to look pretty
    rather than be beautiful.

Must we be identical souls
    in different disguises?
May your voice
    make you unforgettable.

Help us love those
    we find hard to like.
Make the right impression
    and everybody will know.

Talk only with your eyes
    to the conditions of the moment.
A mysterious stillness
    is watching.

Silence of the Night

Life has its gleam
    Of sunshine--
A soul yearning
    For romance..

If he could gratify
    His desires
Solitude was now
    Luxury.

Sweet and innocent
    Flowers that
Would never lose
    Their fragrance.

It gave him
    A curious sensation--
Like listening to music
    By moonlight.